W9-AVM-244

Under the Bodhi Tree

Under the Bodhi Tree

Published and Translated by:

Dharma Realm Buddhist University
Dharma Realm Buddhist Association
1777 Murchison Drive Burlingame, California, 94010-4504 U.S.A
First Edition 2004
12 11 10 09 08 07 06 05 04 03 1 2 3 4 5 6 7 8 9
ISBN: 0-88139-319-3
Printed on non-acid paper in Malaysia, 2004
Addresses of the Dharma Realm Buddhist Association and its branches are listed at the back of this book.

Library of Congress Cataloging-in-Publication Data

Under the Bodhi tree / published and translated by Buddhist Text Translation Society, Dharma Realm Buddhist University, Dharma Realm Buddhist Association. 1st ed.

p. cm.

ISBN 0-88139-319-3 (alk. paper)

1. Gautama Buddha— Juvenile literature. 2. Buddhists— India— Biography— Juvenile literature. I. Buddhist Text Translation Society. II. Dharma Realm Buddhist University. III. Dharma Realm Buddhist Association.

BQ892 .U53 2002
294.3'63— dc21
[B]

2002066577

The Eight Guidelines of The Buddhist Text Translation Society

1. **A volunteer must free him / herself from the motives of personal fame and profit.**

2. **A volunteer must cultivate a respectful and sincere attitude free from arrogrance and conceit.**

3. **A volunteer must refrain from aggrandizing his / her work and denigrating that of others.**

4. **A volunteer must not establish him / herself as the standard of correctness and suppress the work of others with his or her fault-finding.**

5. **A volunteer must take the Buddha-mind as his / her own mind.**

6. **A volunteer must use wisdom derived from Dharma-Selecting Vision to determine true principles.**

7. **A volunteer must request Virtuous Elders in the ten directions to certify his / her translations.**

8. **A volunteer must endeavour to propagate the teachings by printing Sutras, Shastra texts, and Vinaya texts when the translations are certified as being correct.**

Contents

Under the Bodhi Tree

Published and Translated by:

Buddhist Text Translation Society
Dharma Realm Buddhist University
Dharma Realm Buddhist Association
Burlingame, California, U.S.A.

Under the Bodhi Tree

The Buddha-To-Be

Long ago, in a life before now, the Buddha-T0-Be was born in a wealthy family and given the name, Sumedha. When his parents died, they left him all their wealth— mansions, servants, store houses of grain, fields, gardens, ochards, elephants, camels and herds of cattle. Sumedha noticed that at their death, they were were not able to take a single coin with them. He wondered, Is there a Path that leads beyond the sufferings and difficulties of this worldly world? I must find it." And he gave away all his riches and wealth and entered the forest as a hermit. There, he ate wild food and wore clothing made from bark. For days upon days, he sat in meditation absorbed in bliss.

One morning he was roused from bliss by the distant sound of music and by the vibration of thousands of fearless feet. Sitting with his legs folded, he rose high into the air and flew over the forest until he came to a road.

Workers dotted the road as far as the eye could see. Sumedha called down to them. "What's happening? Why do you work so hard like bees? Why is the road being strewn with golden sand and perfumes? Why the cart of flowers of every kind and color?"

"O Wise Sumedha, haven't you heard? Burning Lamp Buddha is visiting our great city," the road workers answered, leaning on their shovels and looking into the brilliant blue sky where Sumedha was hovering.

Speechless with joy, Sumedha descended, grabbed a shovel, and set to work on the muddy road. A Buddha is coming, he thought. A real live Buddha!

Then faintly, then louder came music…drums! And flutes! And strings! And voices! And there up ahead, Sumedha saw Burning Lamp Buddha moving slowly forward, wreathed in ever-changing colors of dazzling light— now blue, now orange, now green, now pink.

"I want to become a Buddha and help all living beings," said Sumedha, and he spread his cape over a muddy spot in the road and lay upon it. Then letting down his long hair, he stretched it out so that it made a bridge over the mud. "Let the Buddha walk on my hair to keep from soiling his feet."

The music stopped. The voices and the laughter of the children stopped. Sumedha slowly opened his eyes. Light surrounded him, and he could faintly hear a voice say, "The hermit, Sumedha, lying here in the mud, has made a great vow."

And standing there among the thousands of monks and nuns, men and women, elders and children, Burning Lamp Buddha made a prediction for Sumedha. "Far, far in the future, you will become a Buddha! Your name will be Siddhartha. You will be born in the city of Kapilavastu. Your mother will be Queen Maya and your father, King Suddhodana. You will leave the palace and sit under the Bodhi tree. When the morning star appears, you will become enlightened."

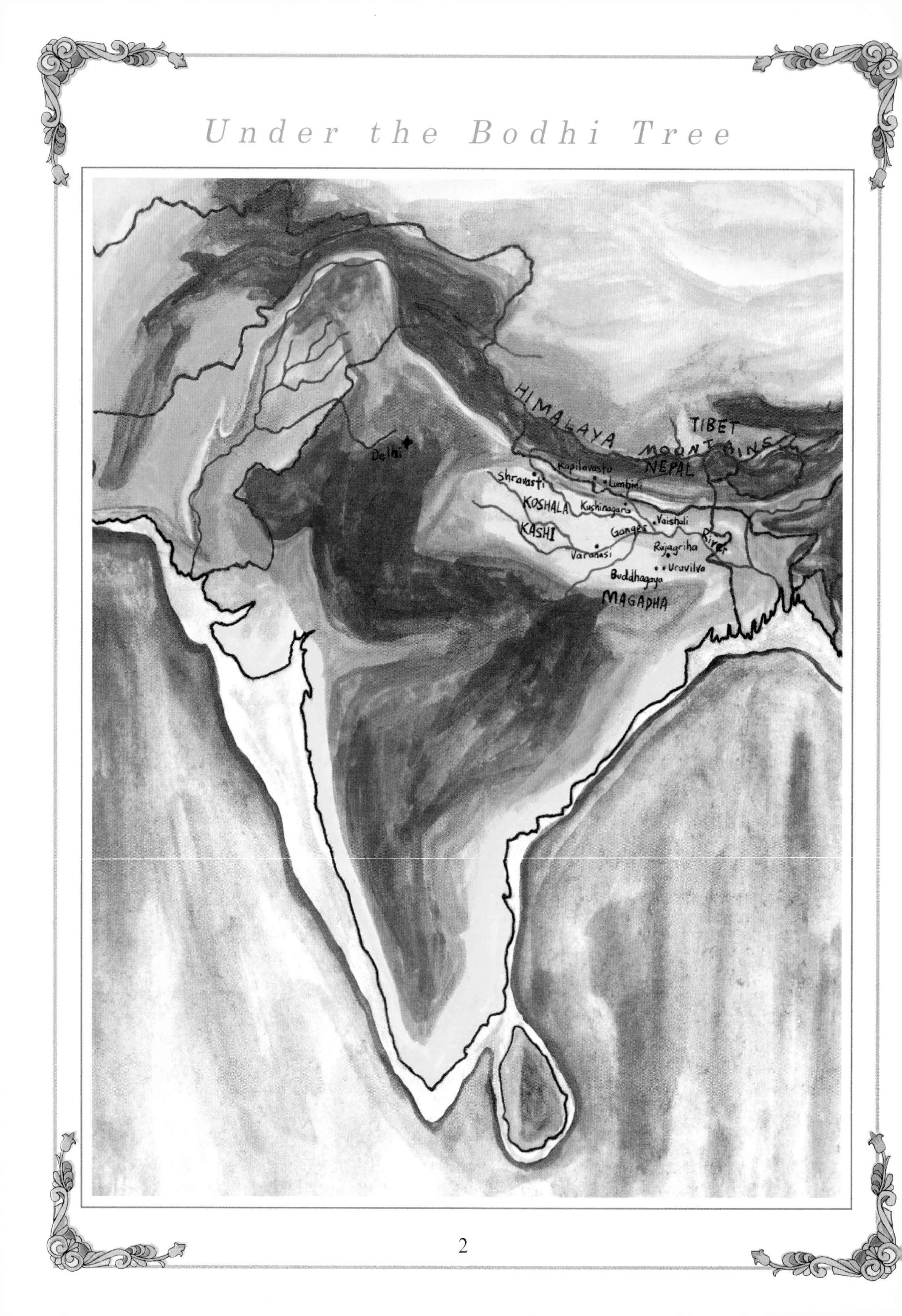
HIMALAYA MOUNTAINS
TIBET
NEPAL
Delhi
Kapilavastu
Lumbini
Shravasti
KOSHALA
Kushinagara
KASHI
Vaishali
Ganges
River
Varanasi
Rajagriha
Uruvilva
Buddhagaya
MAGADHA

With tears of joy, Sumedha knotted his hair on the top of his head and quietly folded up his legs. He flew back into the forest from whence he came. "I, too, will become a Buddha! I, too, shall become a Buddha!" he sang out into the starlight as he soared over the sleeping trees.

Then, in life after life, he was reborn with many different names and in many different places. Joyfully, he worked hard towards his goal until he was reborn in the Tushita Heaven, the Heaven of Happiness. This is where a Buddha-To-Be lives before his last birth.

After a time, the Four Heavenly Kings summoned him. "The moment has come for you to appear in the world and purify the people. Your name will be Siddhartha. You will be born in the city of Kapilavastu. Your mother will be Queen Maya and your father, King Suddhodana. You will leave the palace and sit under the Bodhi tree. When the morning star appears, you will become enlightened."

In a radiant light of brilliant colors, the Buddha-To-Be rode to earth as a white elephant with six golden tusks. The light shone in the nighttime sky like a blazing star.

Far below, from a mountaintop, a sage named Asita gazed at the blazing star. "A Buddha will soon be born in the world," he said.

More than 2,000 years ago in India, where the Snow Mountains rise high above the clouds, there was a small kingdom of the Shakya clan. Although the kingdom was small, it was known for its great wealth, its rich and fertile land, and its just and goodly King Suddhodana and his gentle wife, Queen Maya. Far and wide, because of the vast fields of rice and storehouses of grain, the just and goodly king was known as the White Rice King throughout the land.

Queen Maya Has a Dream

Long, long after Sumedha vowed to become a Buddha, on the night of the Summer Moon Festival, Queen Maya had a dream. In her dream, she was carried through the air by the Four Heavenly Kings to Lake Anavatapta high in the Snow Mountains. The queens of the four kings came and bathed her and dressed her in heavenly clothing. Then she was led to a golden palace on top of a silver mountain.

There, as she lay upon a soft, splendid couch, she was anointed with the finest perfumes and adorned with jewels and garlands of the most brilliant flowers ever seen. Suddenly a comet brighter than the brightest star streaked across the sky, falling silently behind the great mountain. Then into the golden palace where Queen Maya lay, came a magnificent white elephant holding a lotus flower in its great silvery trunk. It trumpeted joyfully. Once! Twice! Three times and circled the queen thrice. Then it touched her right side with the white lotus. When the queen awoke the next morning, she told the king her dream.

And the goodly king summoned sixty-four holy men, the wisest in the land. He honored them with a grand and glorious rice feast in the grand and glorious palace. They were served golden bowls full of honey and clarified butter with sweet rice, curries of all flavors, melons and mangos, and so on. Thereupon, the king gave them wonderful and glorious gifts made from gold and silver, yards of fine white cloth and herds of tawny cattle.

The beautiful Queen Maya told the holy men her dream. She told of the jeweled flowers and the thousand-petal white lotus and of the brilliant light. She told of the magnificent white elephant and how it trumpeted and circled around her. Her voice was gentle and peaceful, and light poured from her face as she spoke.

The goodly and just king closed his eyes and listened once again to the queen's dream. The holy ones sat in rapt attention, taking in each and every word. After the queen had finished speaking, the holy men nodded their heads in knowing wonder. The oldest rose quietly and smiled, "Rejoice, O King! Rejoice! Your beloved queen will bear a son—a son destined for the greatest greatness, a teacher to all." Then the holy ones bowed and took their leave, keeping what they heard a secret that only they could know.

The king was delighted with the good news. "May the music play!" he said. "May the dancers dance! May the drummers drum! May gifts be gifted to everyone throughout the kingdom, to the poor and rich alike!"

The Birth of a Prince

All winter long, the king and queen awaited the birth of their son. In the spring, blossoms washed the air and warm rains melted the snow. Queen Maya said, "The time has come for our child to be born. I must go to my parents' home right away." It was the custom in India for women to return to their family home so their children could be born there.

"So be it!"said the just and goodly king and had the roads leveled and lined with vessels of water and decorated with flowering trees and colorful banners that fluttered in the soft breezes from the hills. He seated the queen in a palanquin, a golden carrying chair, and sent her off with friends and a thousand attendants.

The royal party had not traveled far when they came to the beautiful gardens of Lumbini. The queen said, "Let us stop here and rest amid the flowers."

It was the eighth day of May. The gardens were buzzing with the hum of bees and filled with the sweet scent of sala trees in full bloom. Daylight had begun to fade and a silver moon rose above the treetops. Stretching out her hand, Queen Maya reached up to pluck a flower from the branch of a tree. As she did, the tree bent over for her and the earth gently trembled. At that moment, a shining baby boy was born from her right side. He was as dazzling as the sun in a cloudless sky and was perfect in every way.

The attendants wrapped the child in a royal cloth and presented him to his mother, the queen. The animals danced with joy and the gods rained down precious jewels and garlands of lotus flowers. Two springs gushed up from the earth and two streams of water descended from the heavens— one cool and one warm—refreshing both mother and child. A feeling of peace and happiness spread throughout the world.

Then to the amazment of everyone, the child slipped out of his mother's arms and, like a newborn lion cub, took seven steps. With each step, a brilliant red lotus flower sprang up from the earth beneath his feet. Pointing one finger to the heavens and one finger to the earth, he spoke these words, "In the heavens above and the earth below, I am the World Honored One. In this life, I shall become a Buddha."

After the queen had rested, the royal party returned to the palace with the good news. The king greeted his new son with great rejoicing. "This is the happiest day in my life," he said.

On the fifth day after the birth, the king again summoned the sixty-four holy men, the wisest in the land, to the grand and glorious palace for the naming ceremony of the prince. Each wise man, in turn, gazed silently at each and every feature of the prince and smiled. Then the oldest quietly stood up and said, "His name will be Siddhartha."

The other wise men nodded their heads in knowing agreement and took their leave. The name Siddhartha means "every wish fulfilled."

The Wise Asita

Far, far away in the Snow Mountains, Asita saw a dazzling light shining over the city of Kapilavastu. He knew that a prince had been born. Seated with his legs folded, he rode the rosy clouds of early morning to the palace. The king graciously welcomed him. "What brings you here, my friend?" he asked.

"I have come to see your precious son," said Asita.

Queen Maya held the glowing prince up for Asita to see. Joy and rapture flooded his heart. "Rejoice! O King and Queen, a unique child is born to you," he said. "He has the signs of a great person. A white light shines from between his eyebrows. His body sparkles like gold. There are wheels on the palms of his hands and on the soles of his feet. His arms and legs are long and his eyes are bright like a lotus blossom."

Gazing at the child, Asita, who knew of things to come, went into deep thought. He said, "The prince will become a king of kings. But if he sees the four signs— an old man, a sick man, a dead man and a monk— he will leave the kingdom and become a holy man, a Buddha." Then a tear rolled down his wrinkled, old cheek.

The king was troubled. "Will some misfortune befall the prince?" he asked.

Asita answered, "I foresee no harm for the child. He will be a great teacher and bring peace and happiness to all the world. I weep for myself, for I am old and will not be here to honor and learn from him."

Saying no more, Asita flew back to his cave in the snow-capped mountains whence he came. That night he looked up into the nighttime sky and spoke to the silent stars, "Rare indeed! Rare indeed! A Buddha is born in our land."

The king acted as if he had not heard a word Asita said. "It is not fit for my son to become a holy man," he said to Queen Maya. "I will see that he grows up to be a brave warrior and a mighty king. Together, he and I will rule the land of India."

But Queen Maya had other thoughts. As the moon rose above the palace walls, she gathered her newborn baby in her arms and took a stroll in the royal garden. Watching his face in the light of the moon, she heard and she saw something known only to her. "No, my son," she whispered. "You will not be a king. You will be a Buddha."

On the seventh day after the birth, Queen Maya fell ill and sent for her sister, Prajapati. She said, "My dear sister, soon I will leave this world. After I have gone, please be a kind mother to Siddhartha." Then she passed away. The happiness that the people felt for the newborn prince turned into sorrow at the loss of their beloved queen.

Under the loving care of his aunt, Prajapati, who became the new queen of the Shakya clan, Siddhartha grew up to be a happy child. She treated him as if he were her own child, and he thought of her as his own mother.

Prince Siddhartha's Childhood

Now the goodly king, the child's father, being a king himself and wanting his son to be a king, did everything he could to make Siddhartha's life happy and pleasant. His rooms were made of sweet-smelling wood and his royal robes woven by the finest weavers. He slept on silk cushions and ate the most delicate food. Lovely servants, wearing tiny tinkling bells, waited upon him day and night. And a white umbrella laden with lotus flowers was held over him to protect him from the sun, wind and rain. He even rode in a carriage yoked to two golden deer.

Everything he wished for was his. Yet with all this attention, Siddhartha was not spoiled in the least. He was kind to everyone who waited on him and was a wonder to all.

Hundreds of loving playmates roamed the palace grounds with Siddhartha, but he was most happy when Queen Prajapati and the king gave birth to a son named Nanda, who was the half-brother of Siddhartha. Later, Sundari, his half-sister, was born. Along with Siddhartha, Nanda and Sundari were brought up by their loving parents in a life of luxury and play.

One spring day, when Siddhartha was five years old, the king said to him, "Today is the Annual Plowing Festival held by the old rose-apple tree. You are old enough to go with me this year."

Whips cracked the air! Cowbells clanged! Everyone cheered as the king took the handles of his golden plow decorated with white lilies and streamers. He plowed the first row for spring planting. Next came the royal ministers with their silver plows. Then thousands of peasants took over with their wooden plows. Dripping with sweat, they beat the poor oxen as they bellowed and struggled to pull the heavy plows through the hard earth.

Suddenly the sky darkened and a flock of black birds circled overhead. They swooped down into the freshly turned soil, snapping up the tiny, wriggling worms with their sharp beaks. Siddhartha tugged at his father's sleeve, crying. "Can't someone stop them?"

The king laughed heartily, "No, my son, it's only natural."

But Siddhartha did not laugh. He turned away from the unhappy sight and sat in the shade of the rose-apple tree. Looking around, he saw the beauty of the countryside, the fields and streams and blooming trees. Yet in all this beauty, he saw suffering. A preying mantis was chasing a moth. A snake slid down from the tree and swallowed the preying mantis. And just as suddenly an eagle pounced down on the snake and ate it. Siddhartha asked, "Why must creatures kill each other in order to live? Why must the farmers beat their oxen? Why? Why?"

Sitting quietly in the shade of the rose-apple tree, he closed his eyes and went into a deep meditation, pondering these questions. When the servants came to fetch him, they noticed that the shadow of the tree had not moved since morning. They quickly ran for the king. And when the king saw his son sitting there so peacefully, he marveled in wonder.

Education

Siddhartha awakened early and dressed in a hurry. He was now eight years old and this was his first day of school. After scrubbing his face clean, he ran to the classroom with his long writing stick and slate ready. He was the first there. Hearing his teacher's footsteps coming down the hall, he stood up straight and grinned from ear to ear.

A small man with twinkling eyes entered the room. He bowed to Siddhartha and said, "My name is Visvamitri. I will teach you about the sun in the sky and the stars in the heavens. You will study rocks and learn the calls of birds. I will also teach you to read and write and to play the flute. And good manners, of course."

Before long, the large classroom was filled with five hundred other princes, who would be Siddhartha's classmates. Among them were his cousins, Ananda and Devadatta, and his half-brother, Nanda. The teacher asked the princes many questions, but Siddhartha was the only one who gave answers, each answer better than the one before. The teacher shook his head in wonder and asked himself...who is the teacher and who is the student?

After classes were over every day, Siddhartha's classmates played fighting games in the schoolyard and went hunting for birds and rabbits. "Come play war with us," they called to Siddhartha. "Come hunting with us."

But Siddhartha said, "I would rather explore the woods and play with the little furry animals. They're my friends. I don't want to hurt them."

"You're just afraid to fight," said his cousin, Devadatta, laughing. "You're a coward." But Siddhartha just smiled and wandered off alone.

When the just and goodly king heard about Siddhartha's behavior, he shook his head and said to Visvamitri, "My son is too kind-hearted. I want him to become a strong warrior. Have him trained in the arts of war."

"So be it," said Visvamitri, and he had Siddhartha trained in archery, wrestling and joustling from elephants.

One day the king told Siddhartha, "I have a present for you." He gave a low whistle and out from the shade of a tree trotted a snowy white colt. "This is your horse. Take care of him. He will make a fine horse one day."

"What a wonderful present," said Siddhartha, running his fingers through the colt's long, white mane. "I will call him Kanthaka."

Before Visvamitri gave Siddhartha riding lessons, he taught him how to feed and groom Kanthaka. Soon Siddhartha was riding Kanthaka as swift as the wind, racing across the meadows and jumping fences and wide streams. In the winter, he rode with Visvamitra through the deep snow in the woods, taking food to the starving animals.

The Wounded Swan

One day Siddhartha and Devadatta were practicing archery in the woods by the palace lake. Devadatta was the best archer among the princes and was teaching Siddhartha to shoot at moving objects. He threw a mango into the air and said, "Line up your arrow just in front of the mango and…" Just then, the princes heard the cry of a wild swan as it flew up from the lake. Lowering their bows, they watched in wonder as the great white bird rose gracefully up into the clear blue sky, high above the distant mountains.

Without warning, Devadatta quickly fitted his bow with an arrow. *Swish!* He let the arrow fly. "Don't shoot!" cried Siddhartha. But it was too late. With a sharp cry, the swan tumbled down from the sky and fell to the ground with a thud.

Siddhartha ran and picked up the quivering bird. "Oh, you poor swan," he said, gently stroking it. "Don't be afraid. I'll help you." And he carefully pulled the arrow out of its wing.

Devadatta came running up, panting and shouting, "Hey, that's my swan! Give it to me. I shot it and it belongs to me."

"I'll never give it to you. You'll only kill it," Siddhartha said. "Animals love their lives as much as people do. And they also have families. Who'll take care of the baby swans if the mother dies?"

"I don't care. It's only a bird," said Devadatta.

"We'll never settle this argument," said Siddhartha. "Let's ask the wise men for help."

The wise men in the king's court listened to each prince tell his side of the story. One wise man said, "Devadatta shot the bird, so it belongs to him."

Another said, "But Prince Siddhartha is the son of the king, so the bird should go to him."

The door of the courtroom suddenly opened. In came an old, old man with a beard that nearly touched the floor. No one remembered ever seeing him before. In a laughing voice, the old man said, "The swan should go to the one who will save its life, not to the one who will destroy it." He turned to leave.

"Wait, good sir, who are?" asked the wise men. But the old man just gave a friendly wave and disappeared. No one ever saw him again.

The wise men nodded in agreement. They said, "Without a doubt, the swan should certainly go to Prince Siddhartha."

Wrapping the swan in his shirt, Siddhartha carried it to the palace. There he tended to its wing with herbs and fed it with great care. When it was well enough to fly on its own, he took it to the edge of the lake and let it go free to live with its own kind. Lifting the bird up in the air, he said, "Fly far, far away from here so you will be safe."

Standing behind a tree near the edge of the lake, Devadatta watched the swan disappear into the orange and cranberry colors of sunrise. "Someday I will get even with Siddhartha," he said. A seed of jealousy was planted in his heart.

Prince Siddhartha Chooses a Bride

Siddhartha blossomed into a young man of great strength, beauty and wisdom. Wishing to please his beloved father, he was trained in the duties of the court. For long hours, he sat through talks of war and gaining wealth. He was entertained by musicians and dancers with eyes as bright as jewels who danced with the grace of fairies. But he was simply not interested in court life. He preferred to sit alone in his father's garden, pondering the meaning of life.

Seeing his son so unhappy, the king became frantic with worry. Will Prince Siddhartha leave the palace and become a holy man like Asita? he wondered. Calling his ministers together, he said, "Let there be more music! More dancing girls! Scour the land for acrobats! The best mimes! Rare birds! Rare fish! Make my son happy again."

But the ministers advised him otherwise. "Siddhartha is sixteen years of age and old enough to marry," they said. "With a family, he will surely be happy and stay in the palace forever."

When the king discussed marriage plans with Siddhartha, Siddhartha agreed. He said, "A wife for me does not have to be beautiful. She has to be gentle and kind. And fun."

High above the city of Kapilavastu, the palace bells clanged and clanged. They echoed through the mountain slopes like a thousand bells ringing at once. People rushed to the town square.

"A proclamation!" cried the king's herald as he unrolled a long scroll. "Hear Ye! Hear Ye!" he cried. "Let the Shakyan families send their most beautiful daughters. Prince Siddhartha is ready to choose a bride."

On an appointed day, the king invited all the beautiful young princesses from all the kingdoms in the land to a grand and glorious feast at the grand and glorious palace. The royal families dressed each of their daughters in their loveliest garments and jewels and offered them in marriage to Siddhartha. With all their radiance and charm, one by one, the princesses walked up to him and introduced themselves. Siddhartha presented each one with a jewel. Hundreds of princesses came. But to the king's disappointment, none of them caught Siddhartha's eye.

As Siddhartha rose to take leave, the hall door opened and in rushed a princess named Yashodhara. She was as beautiful and tender as a lotus bud. Smoothing her hair and straightening her bodice, she walked breathlessly up to Siddhartha and curtsied. She asked, "O Prince, is there a gift for me?" The table was empty.

Smiling, Siddhartha removed the ring from his finger and placed it on hers. "O Princess, here is a special gift just for you," he said.

"My son has found the perfect bride," cried the king. "Let the music play! Let the dancers dance! Let the drummers drum! Let gifts be gifted!"

The Royal Contest

But when the just and goodly King Suddhodana proposed marriage between the youths, Yashodhara's father, King Suprabuddha, said, "It is the custom of our clan to marry our daughters to warriors who are brave and wise. Prince Siddhartha lives a life of luxury and is too delicate. What will he do when war breaks out? Let there be a contest to put his strength to the test."

So King Suddhodhana proclaimed seven days of royal contests. On each day of the event, the sports arena was filled with hundreds of noble princes who came to test their skills and to win the hand of Princess Yashodhara. An eager crowd waited for the contests to begin.

The first contest of the first day was in archery. One by one, the noble princes notched their arrows and took their turn, but not one was able to hit the target. When Devadatta stepped up for his turn, the crowd silenced. A wicked grin spread slowly across his face as he held his long bow ready. And being the fine archer that he was, he carefully sited the target and sent his arrow flying straight into the bull's eye.

The crowd roared, "The winner is Devadatta!"

Yashodhara's heart sank. Sitting next to her father in the front row of the arena, she remained silent. She did not want him to know how she felt. But inside she cried, "Where is Siddhartha? I'll die if I have to marry Devadatta."

Suddenly an arrow went flying over the heads of the crowd. It split Devadatta's arrow in two. The crowd cheered! The drums rolled! "It is Prince Siddhartha. He has won!" Yashodhara smiled.

On the following days, there were contests in everything from poetry and math to running and joustling. In academics, his answers silenced the judges. Running as swift as a deer, he took first place. He sliced down a tree with one stroke of his sword. With a mere touch of his pole, in jousting, he knocked his opponents off their elephants, as if they were straws. Riding Kanthaka, he left the others far behind in horse racing.

"It's easy for Siddhartha to win riding Kanthaka," said Devadatta. "Bring out the wild black horse. Let's see who wins!"

Aniruddha was the first to mount the wild-eyed horse. The horse exploded, kicking and bucking, throwing him to the hard ground. Just in time, Nanda pulled him out from under the horse's sharp hooves, saving his life. Other princes tried their luck, but were thrown off like hot coals. When it was Siddhartha's turn, he walked slowly up to the horse, whispering softly. Gently holding onto the mane with both hands, he slid up onto the horse's wet back and rode around the arena, stopping in front of Yashodhara and her father. The crowd cheered, tossing jewels and flowers into the air.

Yashodhara's father said to her, "Prince Siddhartha will make you a fine husband."

The seed of jealousy continued to ripen in the heart of Devadatta. Glaring with hatred at Siddhartha, he sneaked away from the wild crowd.

A Rude Awakening

Siddhartha and Yashodhara lived in a world of nothing but happiness and laughter. Out of joy, the king had three palaces built for them— one for the cool season, one for the hot, and one for the rainy. The palaces were surrounded by flowing fountains and pools of sparkling water, filled with red, white and blue lotus flowers and fish of all the colors in the rainbow.

Moreover, the king had a high wall built around the palace and placed guards at the four gates. "Do not let Prince Siddhartha leave without my permission," he told them. "Old and sick people are not allowed in the palace. Keep holy men far away."

To his servants, he said, "Rake away the dried leaves and pluck the wilted flowers. Siddhartha is not to see even a dead rose!"

With all this, the king thought his worries were over. But he did not know what was in Siddhartha's heart. He did not know of the things that Siddhartha talked about with Yashodhara. "All around me there is beauty and joy, yet I feel like a chained elephant. Are there other joyful things beyond these palace walls? Are there gardens as lovely as these? How do my people live? Tell me!"

One warm summer day, as Siddhartha and Yashodhara were strolling along a path in the garden of the summer palace, they heard a young servant girl singing a song that Siddhartha had never heard. It was a song about the beauties of the world— of waterfalls and oceans and singing seashells, of vast valleys and purple mountains, of golden cities with happy people. He longed to see these wonders.

Going to his father, he asked, "O King, grant me permission to visit the great city of Kapilavastu. I wish to see what lies beyond the palace walls, to see the people that I will someday rule."

The just and goodly king had long been dreading this moment. But he could not refuse his beloved son's wish. "So be it!" he said. "You may go tomorrow morning at the break of day. I will make the necessary arrangements."

With drums and gongs, the king had it proclaimed throughout the kingdom, "Hear Ye! Hear Ye! All you people, sweep the streets. Remove every stick and stone. Strew the roads with flower petals, and perfumes and golden sand. Hang lanterns and fly banners of every size and color. Prince Siddhartha will visit your golden city."

And the king had jewels and garments of the finest silks and brightest colors passed out to the young, beautiful and strong people in the city. "Tomorrow is a holiday," he said. "Lay aside your work. Close the shops. Dance and sing in the streets. Play music and make merry. And remember to keep the old and sick people hidden."

The First Journey

Channa, the charioteer, rose at daybreak the next day and hitched Kanthaka, Siddhartha's horse, to a golden chariot. Taking the reins, Siddhartha drove out of the palace through the East Gate and raced to the city. Garlands of bright flowers hung everywhere. Gaily colorful banners waved in the morning breeze. When the crowds of happy people saw their beloved prince dressed in royal splendor, looking as majestic as a god, they cheered and showered him with flowers and bowed in admiration.

So this is life, he thought. The city sparkles and my people are happy. Then why have I been so sad? "But what, oh, what is that?" Siddhartha cried, pulling up his horse. Kanthaka stopped and pointed his ears back. Suddenly, right before their eyes, an old beggar appeared. His skin was wrinkled, his head bald, and his teeth gone. He tottered from the crowd and stood in the road. "Is it a man or some other kind of creature?" Siddhartha asked.

"That, O Prince, is an old man," said Channa.

"Tell me Channa, do all people get old like that?"

"Yes, O Prince. It cannot be helped," Channa answered.

Siddhartha trembled. "Knowing that one day I will get old, how can I enjoy this pleasure ride?" he said. Wheeling the chariot around, he drove with lightning speed back to the palace.

The Second Journey

The next morning Siddhartha and Channa rose with the sun and drove out the South Gate to tour another part of the city. "Let us see more!" said Siddhartha. Again happy crowds of people cheered and smiled and sprinkled heaps of flowers in his path, casting their admiring eyes upon him. Suddenly a sick man appeared lying on the ground, coughing and moaning in pain. Kanthaka neighed and pawed the ground. "What, oh, what is that, Channa? It looks like a man, but is it?" asked Siddhartha.

"That, O Prince, is a sick man."

"Was he born like that?" asked the prince.

"Most likely he was born as strong as you or me," said Channa. "Everyone gets sick. It's nothing to worry about."

"Nothing to worry about! First the horror of old age and now sickness. How can I go on seeking pleasure?" After finding someone to take care of the sick man, Siddhartha wheeled the royal chariot around and fled back to the palace in despair.

The Third Journey

On the third day, Siddhartha and Channa drove out the West Gate for the city. The royal chariot was splendidly decorated with pure white lotus flowers. And once again, happy crowds cheered and covered their beloved prince with flowers.

Suddenly the sound of wailing shattered the peaceful morning. A group of people came down the road, carrying a man on a stretcher.

"What, oh, what is that, Channa?" cried Siddhartha, dropping the reins. "What is wrong with that man?"

"He is dead," said Channa. "It is the end of his life."

"Will I, the son of the king, also die like this man? And the king and queen and my wife?"

"Everyone will die," Channa gently told the prince. Too shocked for words, Siddhartha drove in silence back to the palace.

Siddhartha could not forget the old man, the sick man and the dead man. He thought about them day and night and could find no peace in his heart. Everything in the palace seemed dead and cold to him. "Now I know what life is like outside the gates," he told Yashodhara. "Everyone appears happy, yet beggars line the streets and children go hungry. The sick and old wait for a lonely death, while the rich live in luxury. Yet no one knows, not even the rich, when old age, sickness or death will strike. Is there no more to life than this? Is there no end to sorrow?"

The Last Journey

For the last time, in the glow of morning light, Channa and Siddhartha set out the North Gate. The smiling crowds, with arms full of garlands, lined the roads. But Siddhartha did not see them. He only saw a man dressed in ragged robes standing by the side of the road, waiting for the chariot to pass. Struck by the glow of light in the man's face, Siddhartha pulled Kanthaka to halt. "What, oh, what is that, Channa? Is it a god or a man?" he asked.

Channa said, "That is a seeker of the Truth, a holy man. He has given up everything and wanders in the forests and mountains."

Siddhartha asked the holy man, "O Venerable One, is there a Path that leads beyond the sufferings and difficulties of this world? Please show me."

The holy man beat on the ground three times with his staff. Then he was gone! Alas, Siddhartha had no one to teach him. "Then I must find the Truth on my own," he said, a river of hope flooding his heart. "I must leave the palace and give up my crown, my riches, my father and my wife and enter the forest. There is no time to lose."

Siddhartha quickly returned to the palace and spoke to the king, "Now that I am twenty-nine years old, I wish to leave the palace to seek the Truth. Please grant me your permission, O King."

"Enough of this! I am your father. How can you leave me?" said the king.

"I see all men as my father and all women as my mother," said Siddhartha. "I want to help everyone."

"Think no more of this! You are in the bloom of youth. If you stay, I will give you all my wealth and the entire kingdom to rule," said the king.

"I will stay if you promise me four things."

"Whatever you wish for is yours," said the king.

"That I will never grow old, get sick or die, or lose my wealth."

Knowing that these promises could never be fulfilled, the goodly king wept and could not be comforted. "Double the guards at the city gates!" he ordered the guards. "Do not let my son escape."

Quickly, Siddhartha slipped into his wife's chambers to tell her of his decision. For a long time, she knew that this day would come. Although she understood her husband's quest for the Truth, now that the time had come, her heart was filled with sorrow. "I ask for only one thing," she said. "That you leave me with a child so I will not be lonely while you are away."

Channa tapped quietly on the door. "Kanthaka is ready!" he whispered. "We must leave the palace at once. "

Siddhartha quickly pointed his finger at Yashodhara, saying, "You will have a son and his name will be Rahula."

Leaving the Palace

In the quiet moonlight, the Four Heavenly Kings appeared and held the hooves of Kanthaka in their hands. Over the palace wall, they lifted him with Siddhartha and Channa riding on his back. And off they rode into the darkness of the nightime sky.

As he left the palace, Siddhartha wanted to have one last look at his beloved city, Kapilavastu. Fearing that he might wish to return, the Four Heavenly Kings quickly turned the earth around like a potter's wheel. When Siddhartha looked back, there was nothing to see.

Suddenly a huge black cloud billowed up in front of Siddhartha, blocking the light of the moon. "Halt!" a voice thundered. "I am Mara, God of Evil, the ruler of the universe. Return to the palace and I will give you the entire universe to rule."

"Out of my way, Mara!" said Siddhartha, spurring Kanthaka onward. "Nothing can stop me from my quest." Bursting through the dark, black clouds, they mounted the milky way, leaving Mara behind in a cloud of star dust.

That night Siddhartha and Channa passed over three great kingdoms. At dawn they alighted in the Snow Mountains far, far away from Kapilavastu.

Resting by a mountain stream, Siddhartha cut off his long princely locks with a single stroke of his sword. Tossing them up into the sky, he said, "Now I begin my quest for the Truth." A heavenly god caught the locks in a golden net and carried them to the Tushita Heaven.

The gods of the forest came out to welcome Siddhartha, presenting him with a yellow rag robe and an offering bowl. After changing into the rag robe, Siddhartha gave his royal garments and crown to Channa, saying, "Quickly, my friend, return to the palace with Kanthaka. Give these to the king and tell him what has become of me."

Channa fell to the ground, begging, "I followed you out of the palace and I was with you when you flew away from the city. Allow me to stay and serve you."

"I must go alone," Siddhartha said thoughtfully, "When I have found the Truth, I will then return to teach you."

Stroking Kanthaka's long white mane, Siddhartha whispered in his ear, "Farewell, old friend. You have served me well."

"Come, Kanthaka!" said Channa, pulling on the reins. But Kanthaka just stood there. A huge tear slid down his cheek and melted into the bridle. Lightly whinnying, he leaned over and licked Siddhartha's feet clean. Then rearing his front legs high up into the air, he turned into a heavenly god and rose up to the Tushita Heaven.

Sobbing, Channa set out alone to break the news of Siddhartha to the royal family.

In the Snow Mountains

For the first time in his twenty-nine years, Siddhartha was alone. He had no palace to live in and no servants to care for him. Wearing a rag robe and carrying his bowl, he wandered from place to place as holy people do in India. But the rag robes did not conceal the beauty of his youth and his majestic manner. The mountain people felt blessed in his presence and happily filled his bowl. In silence, he accepted the food they offered.

A woodcutter led him through the mountains to the Forest of Hermits. The lovely groves were alive with holy people contemplating the mysteries of life and death. Eating little food and wearing rags, they devoted themselves to meditation, yoga, and pure living. Is this where I belong? Siddhartha wondered.

There he found the wise yogi teachers, Arada and Udraka. He sat in turn, at their feet, and learned the wisdom of the Indian religions, but he did not learn how to end suffering. "There is no one in the world who understands that," said the yogis.

"Then I must find the Truth on my own," Siddhartha said and moved on.

Into the deep forest he went alone, never sleeping under the same tree twice. In Uruvilva, he met some hermits who told him, "The best way to end suffering is to overcome fear and bodily pain."

Thinking this was the right path, Siddhartha underwent all kinds of difficult practices for six years. He lived on wild fruit and roots, wearing clothes made from strips of pounded bark. He slept on a bed of thorns and stood on one leg for hours. In the winter, he sat in the icy snow. In the summer, he sat in the blazing sun. No one endured more hardships than he.

At first, he was afraid at night. The snap of a twig, the rustle of a leaf, the cry of a peacock sent his blood curdling. Run! Run! he thought, but he never did. He bravely sat and faced his fear. The animals, admiring his courage, protected him. Deer brought flowers and monkeys came with fruit.

Before long, his fame as a holy man reached the kingdom of Kapilavastu. Five of his friends from the royal family said, "Let us find Siddhartha. He will teach us the Truth." Finding him on the bank of the clear, flowing Neranjara River, they took him as their teacher and followed his ways.

At that time, Siddhartha was eating one grain of wheat and one sesame seed a day. His skin was dried up like a leaf and his bones stuck out like sticks. Queen Maya looked down from the Tushita Heaven and wept for her son. So did the gods.

Siddhartha still forced himself on, sitting in silence. Bugs bit him and scurried across his chest. But he did not move so much as a finger to brush them away, lest he harm them. Layers of dust covered his body. The children of the forest thought he was a dust demon. They threw sticks and mud at him to chase him away. From deep in their sockets, his eyes smiled kindly at them, with no anger.

Unable to bear any more, two of his friends said, "This life is too hard. We'll never become enlightened this way. Let's leave."

An Offering of Milk

Every spring a sparrow came and built its nest on Siddhartha's shoulder. One spring, it did not return. Tears of loneliness filled Siddhartha's eyes. "All these years, I have spent in unspeakable pain, and still there's sadness in my heart," he said. "What's the point?"

But what was that? He sat up straight. The sound of singing voices drifted up from the road, rousing him out of his sadness. A group of girls were singing on their way to the village:

With the strings too loose, the lute does not sound.
With the strings too tight, they will break apart.
Not too loose, not too tight.
The lute sounds just right!

"What a fool I have been!" said Siddhartha. "I have tightened my strings of life too tight. How can I find Truth in a body so lean and wasted? True happiness cannot be found in too much pleasure or in too much pain, but in the middle way."

Leaning on his staff, he made his way to the river to wash away the filth from his body. The water was cool and refreshing, and the sandy bottom felt pleasant under his feet. But after bathing, he was so weak that he almost fainted. A tree spirit bent down a limb so Siddhartha could grab it and pull himself up onto the bank. Tired and weary, he rested under an old banyan tree.

The gods, who were watching over him, were bewildered. "We must help Siddhartha! He's in trouble," they said. Summoning Sujata, a heavenly maiden, they sent her into the forest where she found a lotus flower bearing a jeweled bowl of milk. Finding Siddhartha under the banyan tree, she offered him the milk, then set aside.

He drank in silence and then smiling at Sujata, he said, "If you hadn't given me food, I would have died without finding the Truth. May happiness and good fortune be yours."

When his three friends saw him drinking the rich milk, they became disgusted and said, "Siddhartha has gone back to an easy life. We shall also leave." And they did.

With his renewed strength, Siddhartha stood up, put the empty bowl afloat in the river and said, "If I am to become a Buddha, may this bowl float upstream." And it did. The bowl cut its way against the current and was caught up in a whirlpool. Down, down, it whirled and whirled to the jeweled chambers of the Dragon King, Muchalinda.

Catching the bowl, Muchalinda held it up and announced "Prince Siddhartha will become a Buddha. Let us rejoice!" At these words, the sky turned bright gold and the great golden-winged Garuda bird swooped down into the swirling water. Snapping up the bowl, he took it to the Tushita Heaven. And the river spirits came and sprayed the Buddha-To-Be with showers of emeralds, sapphires, diamonds and other fabulous jewels that fell in a sparkling heap at his feet.

An Offering of Kusa Grass

Once again, Siddhartha began to eat every morning. Soon his golden skin glowed with health. The children from the village were no longer afraid of him. They gathered around him in the afternoons, bringing him offerings of rice-milk and flowers and coconuts that they had gathered from the forest. He told them stories about his search for enlightenment and taught them to be kind to each other. And they understood, each in his or her own way.

On a full-moon day in May, Siddhartha bade the children farewell and went to the river crossing. The jade green waters of the Neranjara River foamed and swelled as the Naga King Muchalinda emerged from his palace on the river bottom. Stretching out his long, thick body covered with silver and turquiose jeweled-scales, he arched up like a rainbow, forming a bridge upon which Siddhartha walked across.

On the road to the city of Gaya, he met a poor young boy named Svasti, who was sobbing bitterly. On his back was a bundle of kusa grass. When he saw Siddhartha, he ran to hide, but Siddhartha blocked his way. Svasti stood dumbstruck.

"Why are you crying, my friend?" Siddhartha asked.

"O Holy One, stay back!" Svasti cried, backing away. "I'm an untouchable."

Siddhartha put his hands on Svasti's shoulder, saying, "I asked not what caste you are, but why you are unhappy?"

Never had Svasti been treated with such understanding. A strange feeling came over him. No longer afraid, he dried his tears and asked, "Have you seen my cows? They ran away while I was cutting grass. Their owner will surely beat me for this!"

"Come, I will help you," said Siddhartha. They walked down to the river where Siddhartha cut a reed and made a flute upon which he played. Sweet notes filled the quiet forest. By and by, he and Svasti could hear the sound of cowbells.

"Look, the cows have come back!" said Svasti. Picking up a stick, he began to beat them. "I'll teach you to run away, dumb beasts!" The eyes of the cows widened and the woods echoed with their loud cries as they felt the sting of Svasti's stick. Again they ran away from him.

Siddhartha said, "Put the stick down. Beating animals turns them away from you and fills them with mistrust and anger."

Filled with shame, Svasti took the flute that Siddhartha handed him and played. Hearing the music, the cows calmed down and returned.

Then Svasti handed a bundle of the sweet-smelling grass to Siddhartha. "Here, this is for you and the lesson you taught me," he said.

Under the Bodhi Tree

In the soft light of the late afternoon, Siddhartha spread the sweet kusa grass under the boughs of a lovely old fig tree. He sat down with his legs crossed and said, "Even if my blood dries up and my skin and bones waste away, I will not leave this spot until I find the way to end suffering."

Now Mara, the Evil One, had been following Siddhartha every step of the way, waiting to catch him in an evil thought or deed. When he heard this vow, he cried out in his booming voice, "I've got to stop Prince Siddhartha! If he becomes enlightened, I'll be doomed." Summoning his armies of demon sons and daughters, and grandsons and granddaughters, he mounted a magnificent elephant and made war on the silent figure.

First, he sent his army of beautiful daughters to lure Siddhartha away from his virtuous path and make him want to return to the palace. They were a vision of loveliness as they twirled and swayed before Siddhartha. Their songs were as sweet as nightingales, their eyes sparkled like sapphires and their faces shone like the moon. Thoughts of the luxurious palace life and the beauty of his wife, Yashodhara, passed across Siddhartha's mind like clouds, but he had no desire to return.

As he sat there, he gazed upon Mara's daughters with a heart of great compassion, knowing that one day they would be old and wrinkled like chicken skin. Under his gaze, the cunning ways of the daughters melted away and their hearts became kind and warm. Running back to their father, they begged him to stop the war.

Mara shook with rage and sent them off. "I'll not quit until Prince Siddhartha is dead!" he shouted. Twirling his magic stick in the air, he conjured up whirlwinds, hail and rain. Clouds of darkness swept across the sky and violent winds lashed at Siddhartha's body. Trees crashed all around him and the earth cracked open at his feet. But the rain did not wet him. The wind did not ruffle the sleeve of his robe. The skies cleared and the storm drifted away. Such was the virtue of Siddhartha—the Buddha-To-Be!

"I must win!" cried Mara and dispatched his frightful army of sons and grandsons. Horrible beasts they were, with human heads, three horns and six eyes. Some were serpents with yellow fangs and stinging tails. Others were monkeys with spider-like fingers. On they came, hissing and screeching. They shot poisoned arrows. They swung chains. They heaved cannon balls and meteors. But as the dreadful weapons came near Siddhartha, he protected himself with a shield of loving kindness. The weapons turned into flower petals and floated to the ground. The meteors became clouds of incense and trailed away into thin threads of smoke. One by one, Siddhartha met Mara's armies and defeated them with his goodness.

Enlightenment

The night became still and peaceful. A full moon crept over the horizon and a mist of tiny red blossoms dropped on Siddhartha's golden shoulders. He went into deep meditation.

Like an eagle soaring to the sun, his mind passed beyond the limits of human understanding. He saw the world as it really is, not the way it appears. He saw the round of birth and death that all living beings keep making. One birth, fifty births, a hundred births, a zillion births. It was the same for everyone and everything— from a tiny ant to the greatest king. All living beings that are born, live and die— not once, but over and over. The cycle is like a wheel that turns round and round. It is called the "Wheel of Rebirth."

He saw that those who do good deeds are reborn into happiness, and those who do evil are reborn into misery, as a beggar, a slave, or even a mouse. That is known as the law of "karma." For every action, there is a result.

He saw that suffering was due to selfish desire and ignorance. The more one has, the more one wants. But when desire and ignorance are ended, suffering vanishes like night. The light of true happiness shines forth, bringing enlightenment. Then one need never be reborn and suffer again.

As the morning star appeared in the sky, Siddhartha opened his eyes and looked at the world through the eyes of a Buddha. He was perfect in wisdom and compassion. He had found the path that leads beyond all the sufferings and difficulties of this world. "Wonder of wonders!" he said. "All living beings have the Buddha nature and can become Buddhas. They only have to follow the Path that I have taken. I will show them the Way."

And on that glorious morning with its glorious light, both gods and humans rejoiced. The blind could see. The deaf could hear. The lame could walk. Dry rivers flowed with water and flowers bloomed out of season. Musical instruments played by themselves. People stopped quarreling and spoke kindly to each other. White light flooded the entire universe and a sweet fragrance permeated the air for miles around.

Bathed in the brilliant light of ever-changing colors— now blue, now orange, now green, now pink— Siddhartha, the Buddha sat in perfect peace. His hair curled to the right and a flesh mound appeared on top of his head, emitting rays of light into the world. And a soft breeze lifted the leaves of the fig tree, now called the Bodhi tree.

Once again Mara appeared, saying, "O Prince! You, who have wasted your life in pleasure and in senseless pain, who will believe that you are enlightened?"

The seated Buddha touched the ground with his right hand. The earth thundered, "I, the earth, am his witness."

The Deer Park

The Buddha gazed at the Bodhi tree, and thanked it for giving him shelter. Then he left the quiet forest to go forth and teach. "Who will accept my teachings?" he asked. "My old teachers, Arada and Udraka are dead. Perhaps my five friends, who were with me in the Snow Mountains, will understand. They have only a little dust in their eyes."

After days of walking, the Buddha crossed the Ganges River and came to the Deer Park near the city of Benares. The park, long adorned with flowering trees, was filled with the songs of birds and the scent of sala flowers. The five friends, seeing Siddhartha enter the park, whispered among themselves, "Here comes Siddhartha, that luxury-loving fellow. Let's ignore him."

As the Buddha came nearer, they saw that he was different. He was surrounded by a radiant light and walked as if in the air. Before they knew it, they forgot their promise and prepared a seat for him and washed his feet. The Buddha said, "I have discovered the Truth— the Path to happiness. If you listen and practice yourselves, you will know that what I say is true."

As the full moon rose on that hot July night, the Buddha gave his first teaching known as "Turning the Dharma Wheel." He spoke these Four Noble Truths:

In life, there is suffering.
The cause of suffering is selfish desire.
Cutting off desire leads to the end of suffering.
The way to end suffering is to follow the Eightfold Noble Path: right views, right thought, right speech, right action, right livelihood, right effort, right mindfulness and right concentration.

The five friends realized that Siddhartha had become an enlightened Buddha and they became the first Buddhist monks. This was the beginning of the Buddhist community known as the Sangha. The Sangha grew and soon there were sixty monks. The Buddha taught them meditations to purify the body, speech and mind. He gave them rules about wearing their robes and taking their daily food, which was vegetarian. Whenever a wrong was done, he made a rule at once, so it would not happen again. These rules became known as Precepts. And the teachings of the Buddha became known as the Dharma.

After three months of training in the forest, the Buddha said, "O monks, go forth for the happiness of the many. Teach this Dharma which is wonderful in the beginning, wonderful in the middle and wonderful in the end. Let each go a different way."

Joyfully, the disciples set out in all directions, walking from village to village. They slept under the stars at night and braved all sorts of weather and hardship. All they asked for was a little food on the way. Their only possessions were a bowl, a robe, a sitting cloth, a needle, a water strainer and a razor. Everywhere they went, they turned the Dharma Wheel, giving people comfort and happiness.

Saving a Lamb

News of the Buddha's teaching traveled fast. Day by day, the number of disciples in his Sangha increased. On one day, a thousand fire worshippers became monks. Following the Buddha to the city of Rajariha, they overtook a herd of sheep being driven down the road.

Among the herd was a little lamb that was being crowded out near a riverbank. Suddenly, it slipped and lost its balance. Down, down it went, tumbling into the river. The strong current bore it swiftly away. "Baaa! Baaa!" it cried out for help.

Hearing the cries, the Buddha leaped into the swirling water and swam to the drowning lamb. Lifting it up on his back, he carried it safely back to the road.

"Where are you taking these sheep?" he asked the sheepherder.

The sheepherder said, "To be sacrificed by King Bimbisara in a fire-worshipping ceremony."

"We will follow you," said the Buddha. And he and the thousand new monks accompanied the herd to the royal palace where the fire ceremony was being held. A huge fire was burning on the altar and a priest was raising a sword to kill the first sheep. Without hesitation, the Buddha stepped in front of the sword and held up his hand. The sword clattered to the ground. Facing King Bimbisara, the Buddha said, "O King, the way to happiness does not lie in the killing of animals."

The king looked from the lamb to the Buddha. His face softened. "Your words have touched my heart," he said. "What you say is true. I will stop this useless killing of animals. From now on, animal sacrifices are forbidden in my kingdom."

The following day, King Bimbisara invited the Buddha to his golden palace to teach the Dharma. The king and the multitudes in his court sat in silence, listening attentively to every word. Afterwards, the king said, "It is my wish that you stay in my kingdom and teach my people. There is a quiet bamboo grove near the city. I will build shelters where you and the monks can live. Will you accept this gift?"

"This is a fine offering," said the Buddha. "The shelters will keep the monks dry and free from illness during the rainy season. And we can avoid stepping on the worms and bugs that fill the roads when it rains."

The grove became the first Buddhist Monastery. It was called the Bamboo Grove Monastery. The Buddha and his monks stayed in the shelters for the three-month rainy season. After the rains were over, they continued to wander, sleeping under the stars.

Soon afterwards, another monastery called the Jeta Grove was presented to the Buddha, then another called the Great Grove and many more. Most of the Buddha's journeys took place between the monasteries as he wandered from place to place, spreading the Truth.

The Return to the Palace

When the Buddha's father, the White Rice King, heard his son was enlightened, he called Channa, "Go to Siddhartha and tell him that his father wishes to see him." Channa found the Buddha in the Bamboo Grove and delivered the king's message.

"Very well, I will visit him," said the Buddha. Happy to see his old servant, he asked Channa, "Would you like to become a monk?"

"But I am a lowly slave, how can I?" asked Channa.

The Buddha said, "Everyone in my Sangha is treated the same, whether one is a king or a slave." With great joy, Channa, at last, became a monk, serving everyone as if they were the Buddha.

At the end of the rainy season, the Buddha and his disciples set out barefoot on the mud-caked road leading to Kapilavastu. By hanging onto the tails of cows, they crossed the wide rivers swollen with melting snow from the Snow Mountains. After two months, they arrived at the Banyan Park outside the city gate, where the king had shelters made for them.

As the Buddha crossed the Rohini River bridge into the city, he stopped at the scene before his eyes. His kinsmen lined the road, holding flowers, perfume and jewels, eagerly waiting. Brightly clad children ran to greet him, playing flutes and waving colored banners in the air.

Tears filled the eyes of the old king when he saw the Buddha, his lotus-eyed son, standing there as perfect as the full moon. Walking slowly up to the Buddha, he placed a garland of flowers around his neck and bowed. The crowd cheered joyously. Their happiness rained down upon the Buddha and their beloved king as they tossed jewels and flowers into the air. One by one, they fell upon their knees until the last jewel clinked on the ground.

The Buddha and his father, the king, met together as they used to in the grand and glorious throne room. The scent of roses drifted in from the garden. The king looked at his precious son sitting next to him, as dear to him as life itself, and questioned him, "When you were a prince, you wore soft silk slippers. Now you walk barefoot on dirt roads. Do your feet hurt?"

"I have given up all desire for an easy life. I feel no pain," said the Buddha.

"You once bathed in rose-scented water. How do you bathe now while roaming around?"

"I bathe in the streams of goodness and virtue."

"In the palace, you slept on soft pillows. Does your body ache from sleeping on the ground?"

"I am peaceful and do not worry about anything. I sleep well and happily."

"You were safe in the palace. Are you afraid at night amid the hooting owls and howling jackals?"

"Such creatures do not frighten me."

"All this could be your kingdom."

"The whole earth is my kingdom. Everyone is my disciple," the Buddha said.

The king looked at the Buddha for a long time, then his eyes brightened. "Wise and true are your words," he said. "I once wanted you to be a mighty king, but now I'm happy that you left the palace and returned as a Buddha."

Yashodhara Tells the Truth

Then the Buddha asked. "Where is Yashodara?"

"She waits for you in her chambers," said Queen Prajapati.

The king then spoke, "When Yashodara heard that you were wearing yellow robes, she began to wear yellow robes. When she heard that you were taking only one meal a day, she began to take only one meal a day. When she heard that you were sleeping on the ground, she began to sleep on a straw mat."

"I have a story to tell you," said Queen Prajapati. "Rahula, your son, was born six years after you left the palace, the same night you became enlightened. The king was mortified. 'How shameful!' he cried. 'My son left home six years ago, how could a prince be born today?' He asked the members of the Shakya clan what to do.

"They said, 'The shameless Yashodhara should be thrown into a fire pit and burned to death.'

"All in the palace agreed except for one servant, who said 'I was with the princess everywhere she went. She did no wrong.' But no one believed her.

"So a fire pit was dug and wood placed in it to burn. With Rahula in her arms, Yashodhara faced the fire and said to everyone, 'My son is indeed born of Prince Siddhartha. If I am telling the truth, when I jump into the fire, neither Rahula nor I will be harmed!'

"Saying this, Yashodhara threw herself into the burning pit. And to our surprise, the pit turned into a pool of clear water. She rose, sitting on a lotus flower, holding Rahula close to her heart. Everyone realized that they had made a mistake and that the birth of Rahula was special."

After the story, the Buddha visited the royal chambers of the princess. When Yashodhara saw him, she fell at his feet and wept with joy. He praised her virtue, saying, "You have been a faithful and devoted wife to me not only in this life but also in many past lives."

During his visit to Kapilavastu, the Buddha ordained 500 Shakyan princes as monks. Among them were his half-brother, Nanda, and his cousins, Aniruddha, Devadatta and Ananda.

In a splendid procession, the royal princes left the city wearing yellow robes and carrying only offering bowls. Following the Buddha, they arrived at the Bamboo Grove with the first clouds of the rainy season.

On the way back, the Buddha stopped at the city of Gaya. On the edge of the city were the poor huts of the untouchables who did the lowest kind of work—tending cows, spreading cow dung and carrying water. There he found Svasti in the stables, building a fire to keep the mosquitoes away from the cows on that hot summer night. "Do you want to give up this wretched life and follow me?" the Buddha asked.

"Yes, World Honored One," said Svasti.

"Then rise and follow me," said the Buddha. And Svasti, the untouchable, rose and followed him to the Bamboo Grove.

The Buddha Teaches Rahula a Lesson

Over the years, the Buddha traveled to Kapilavastu many times to visit his family. His son, Rahula, followed him everywhere. One day he followed him out the palace gate to the Banyan Grove Monastery where the Buddha was staying. The king and Yashodhara, Rahula's mother, did not stop him.

The Buddha asked Rahula, "Would you like to leave the home life and seek the Truth, the greatest happiness known to humankind?"

Rahula replied eagerly, "Yes, World Honored One, I would!" and donned the yellow robe of a monk.

When the king heard that his grandson had become a monk, he was broken-hearted. He asked the Buddha, "Why did you take my grandson without asking me first?"

Realizing his mistake, the Buddha said, "The king has spoken wisely. From now on, everyone has to have permission from their parents to leave the home life."

As the youngest monk, Rahula was adored and spoiled by everyone. He was a holy terror! He did not follow the rules and did just as he pleased. During meditation, he made funny, screeching noises to disturb the monks. And just for the fun of it, he hid the monk's bowls and told lies. "Your hut's on fire," he would tell them. "There's a snake in your room."

When the Buddha heard about Rahula's mischief, he paid him a visit. Happy to see his father, Rahula offered him a basin of water to wash his feet. After washing his feet, the Buddha pointed to the water and asked, "Will you drink this water?"

"No, it's filthy!" said Rahula.

"People who tell lies are just like this water," said the Buddha. "Their minds are unclean." Then he tipped the basin over and the water flowed out onto the floor. "Can this basin now hold water?"

"No, it's useless," said Rahula, as he watched the water trickle out.

"Liars are like this basin," said the Buddha. "They are useless and cannot hold the Truth. No matter how wonderful the Buddha's teachings, and no matter if they wear the yellow robe of the monk, they are of no use. If they do not speak the truth and live a noble life, they will not be fit to do noble work. When they die, no one will feel the loss."

Tears of shame filled Rahula's eyes. From then on, he never told another lie. He was well mannered and eager to learn. Every morning he threw a handful of dirt high up into the air and cried out, "Today, may I learn as many lessons from my teachers as these grains of dirt." Rahula became one of the Buddha's wisest disciples.

The First Nun

One morning as the Buddha sat in meditation on Vulture Peak, he saw with his heavenly eye that his father was lying sick on his bed. "The White Rice King, our father, is sick. We should go visit him before his death," he told Nanda.

Nanda said, "It is right that we go see our father and express our gratitude for his kindness in raising us."

"The king is my uncle," said Ananda. "It was he who allowed me to leave the palace and become the Buddha's disciple. I wish to go with you."

Rahula said, "Although the Buddha is my father, my grandfather, the White Rice King, raised me. I wish to go and attend upon him."

And they went and cared for the just and goodly king, washing and feeding him with love and tenderness. With the Buddha and his family by his bedside, the king passed away in peace. When his body was put in a coffin, the Buddha stood at one end. "To carry a coffin is the duty of the servants," said Nanda.

The Buddha replied, "In the future, people will not be good to their parents. They will not know how to repay their kindness. I will carry my father's coffin to show them the right way."

Nanda, Ananda and Rahula said, "We will help you." As they lifted the coffin onto their shoulders, the earth quaked in six wondrous ways and flowers fell from the heavens in praise of this act of kindness.

After the king's death, Queen Prajapati said to the Buddha, "It would be good if the Buddha would allow women to follow him the same as the monks. They can help the Dharma in womanly ways."

The Buddha said, "The life we lead is not safe for women. It is not necessary to give up your home and family to live a spiritual life. The Buddha's teachings can be followed anywhere." Then the Buddha set out for Vaishali to stay in the Great Grove Monastery for the rainy season.

But Queen Prajapati would not be discouraged. Along with Yashodhara, Sundari and women of the court, she cut off her hair, put on a yellow robe, and headed for Vaishali.

When the women arrived, they were covered with dust and their feet were swollen. Weeping quietly, Queen Prajapati stood outside the gate of the Great Grove. Ananda saw her waiting there. "O Queen Prajapati, why are you waiting...and crying?" he asked, surprised.

"Because the World Honored One will not allow women to be ordained, O Venerable Ananda," she said, wiping away her tears.

"Wait here," Ananda told her. "I'll ask him myself." Ananda asked the Buddha to ordain women. One time, two times, thrice, he asked. Each time, the Buddha refused.

Next time, Ananda asked in a different way, "World Honored One, are women able to attain the same level of spiritual enlightenment as men?"

The Buddha answered, "Yes, Ananda, they can—even in this very life. I will ordain Prajapati. Then she can ordain the other women." Thus Prajapati became the first Buddhist nun. The Buddha was among the first to give women a place in religion.

A Beauty that Never Fades

Vaidehi, the queen of King Bimbisara, was beautiful like the glimmer of moon light on still water. Her lips were smooth as a rose petal and her eyes sparkled like diamonds. The king often said to her, “Come with me to the Bamboo Grove Monastery and meet the Buddha.”

But the queen would say, “I prefer the lovely surroundings and pleasures of the palace. Surely, the royal gardens are more beautiful than the Bamboo Grove.”

“In that case, I will bring the beauty of the bamboo forest to you,” said the king. And he did just that. He had poets compose poetry about the loveliness of the Bamboo Grove--the scent of wild jasmine, the whisper of wind blowing through the swaying bamboo and the lovely songs of birds. The queen, who loved the beauties of nature, was so enchanted by the poems that she decided to visit the grove after all.

One cool, breezy morning, dressed in a gown of blue silk brocade and glittering jewels, the queen was carried in her golden palanquin to the gate of the monastery. She entered the grove alone and strolled along the moss-covered path. The soft pearly light of early morning lit up the path and glimmered on the translucent wings of dragon flies as they skirted back and forth across the tiny trickling streams of cool water. As she stepped across a stream, she heard the sound of a voice from far away, beckoning her. The voice was sweeter than the songs of birds and happier than a babbling brook. Following the voice, she came to a meadow where deer grazed and peacocks strutted with their lovely fan of feathers gleaming in the sun. There, sitting underneath a flowering tulip tree, was the Buddha speaking to a gathering of a thousand monks. Seeing her, the Buddha used his spiritual powers and created a beautiful young maiden who appeared standing by his side, fanning him.

The queen gasped with delight. So enthralled was she by the beauty of the maiden. “Never have I seen anyone so lovely,” she said. “She is as beautiful as a lotus blossom—much more beautiful than I.”

But as the queen came closer, the beauty of the lovely maiden began to fade away. Wrinkles appeared on her skin and her teeth fell out, one after the other. Her hair turned gray, then white. Older and feebler she grew until she sank lifelessly to the ground, disappearing in the dust.

A veil was lifted from the eyes of the queen. Hiding her face in horror, she cried, “If such a body comes to an end like this, then I, too, will lose my beauty and become old and ugly.”

Pitying her, the Buddha said, “Physical beauty does not last. One who is attached to it is like a spider trapped in its own web. There is no way out.”

“I have been vain and selfish all my life,” the queen said. “Now I realize that the only beauty that lasts is the Truth.”

She asked King Bimbisara for permission to join the Order of Nuns and became one of the Buddha’s chief female disciples.

Nalagiri, the Elephant

Over the years the seed of jealousy blossomed in Devadatta's heart. In spite of all his training as a monk, he simply could not tame his own jealousy. "Everyone honors the Buddha and ignores me," he said. "I am his cousin and should be the Buddha myself."

And with his terrible twisted and wicked mind, he plotted to kill the Buddha.

"Nalagiri, the mad elephant!" he cried. "I will have Nalagiri kill the Buddha for me. What a perfect plan." Nalagiri was King Bimbisara's mighty tusker. Like Devadatta, she had a bad nature and could not be tamed.

With a jug of liquor, Devadatta went to the king's stables and said to the elephant keeper, "I will make you rich if you help me." Then he told him his wicked plan.

"So be it, sir!" said the elephant keeper, and he emptied the jug in Nalagiri's drinking trough.

The next morning, the elephant keeper turned Nalagiri out along the road where the Buddha was walking. Cries and screams filled the city. "Nalagiri is loose! Run for your life."

A cloud of dust rose up in front of the Buddha and parted. Out stepped Nalagiri, maddened with liquor. When she saw the Buddha, she trumpeted and rushed towards him. Her tail was stretched out behind her and her eyes were ablaze with fire. The crowds screamed wildly and ran to safety. Only Ananda stood by the Buddha's side.

Raising his hand, the Buddha said, "Come, my friend. Do not be wild and reckless. Do no harm to anyone." Like a ray of sunlight, the power of his loving kindness enveloped her. The noble elephant staggered and stopped, her huge ears fanning back and forth. Her wild eyes softened and huge tears rolled down her old, wrinkled cheeks. Her knees buckled under her as she sank slowly to the ground at the Buddha's feet, bowing. The Buddha then led her back to her stable where she stood in her place, as tame as a lamb.

Unlike Nalagiri who found peace, Devadatta became more cruel and wicked. Still determined to kill the Buddha, he hired a band of archers to shoot him. But the archers were so moved by the Buddha's compassion that they dropped their bows and became his disciples, instead.

Undefeated, Devadatta rolled a boulder off a cliff on the top of the Buddha's head. But before it crushed the Buddha, it broke into tiny pieces. However, one of the pieces cut the Buddha's foot, causing it to bleed.

The Buddha said, "One who sheds the Buddha's blood will die a violent death." When Devadatta heard the Buddha, he turned to run but it was too late. The ground underneath him cracked open and the licking flames of hell pulled him under.

The Buddha said to his disciples, "Devadatta was as dear to me as my own son. After a hundred thousand years in the hells, he will make good his evil ways, rise and become a Buddha named Heavenly King Buddha.

The Last Words

Many memorable events took place in the Buddha's life. Some were happy. Some were sad. Yet the Buddha faced each one of them with great understanding and courage. For forty-five years, he trudged across the rich valleys and parched plains of Northern India. The soles of his feet became like leather and his hair turned gray. Wherever he went, words of wisdom flowed from his lips like sweet dew falling upon the earth in the early morning. "Delight in doing good deeds and giving to the poor. Cherish all life and do not kill. Take only what is given and speak the truth. Conduct yourself well and leave wine and harmful drugs alone. Stay on the road to goodness and good health."

A friend and teacher to all, the Buddha lived only for the sake of others. Now that he was eighty years old, he felt that his work was done. He called the faithful Ananda to him and said, "Let us return to Kapilavastu. I wish to die in the city where I grew up."

Hearing this, tears poured from Ananda's eyes like rain. The Buddha comforted him saying, "Do not grieve, Ananda. I am old and fe eble and cannot live forever. It is natural for everything that is born to die."

On the way to Kapilavastu, the Buddha fell ill in a sala grove outside the village of Kusinagara. Pointing to twin sala trees, he said to Ananda, "Please fold my upper robe and lay it between those trees so I can lie down with my head to the north. I am weary and need to rest a while."

Weeping, Ananda spread out the robe underneath the boughs of the trees on a smooth slab of stone. The Buddha lay on his right side with one knee folded over the other leg, the way a lion lies. As he did so, the trees broke out into full bloom, out of season, and sprinkled white blossoms upon the ragged robes of the reclining Buddha.

The Buddha said, "Ananda, this very night, I will pass into Nirvana, the ultimate peace. In the future, there will be a Buddha named Maitreya who will appear in the world. Now go tell everyone that the Buddha is about to leave so they can come and bid him farewell."

When the people heard the news, they rushed to see the Buddha before it was too late. Even as he lay there in pain, he continued to teach them until his last breath.

The night was almost over and so was the life of the Buddha. The disciples wept and begged him to remain in the world. Ananda asked, "When the Buddha is no longer in the world, who will teach us?"

"What more is there to teach, Ananda?" the Buddha asked. "I have taught you all I know. There is nothing that I have kept hidden. The precepts are now your teacher. Follow them and you will be true to me."

In the purple shadows of dusk, the Buddha entered final Nirvana. Before his departure, he spoke his last words. "All things in life change and decay, but the Truth remains forever. Strive on diligently without delay."

A Day in the Life of the Buddha

The Buddha rose at four o'clock in the morning. After bathing in a cool mountain stream, he sat in meditation, casting his net of compassion out into the world. If anyone needed his help, he went to them. Otherwise, whenever it was light enough to see his hand when he held it up, he took his offering bowl and walked to the nearest village to collect offerings of food. His disciples followed along in single file.

When the people in the villages saw him coming, they cried, "Today, the Buddha has come to our village for offerings." And they came out of their houses and waited on the road, holding incense, flowers, and vessels of food. With happy voices, they bowed and greeted the Buddha and placed food in his bowl.

After the Buddha had finished his meal, he looked into the hearts of the people and taught them what they needed to know. Each felt as if he were speaking especially to him or her. Taking leave of the village, he returned to where he was staying.

At noon the monks and nuns met with the Buddha. He answered their questions and gave them advice on meditation. After his instructions, each went on his own to meditate under a tree or on a riverbank. If the Buddha wished, he rested for a while inside his fragrant hut.

In the afternoon, hundreds of men, women and children from the villages came to listen and seek his advice. After they left, kings and royal families came to discuss their problems. The Buddha encouraged them to stop their wars and to rule their kingdoms peacefully.

At the first watch of the night from six to ten in the evening, the monks or nuns came again to ask questions. In the middle watch, from ten to two at night, the gods and spirits came to hear the Buddha's teachings of wisdom. In the last watch, from two to three in the early morning, the Buddha took a stroll under the moonlight, pacing back and forth, to relieve his body from so much sitting. Then he slept one hour before beginning a new day.

Glossary

BODHI TREE- A sacred fig tree under which Shakyamuni Buddha became enlightened.
DHARMA- A rule or method; the Buddha's teachings and the practice of them.
ENLIGHTENMENT- Understanding the ultimate Truth and thereby attaining freedom from ignorance and desire.
FOUR HEAVENLY KINGS - Gods who abide in the first heaven of the desire realm and protect the Buddhas and their teachings.
GARUDA - In Indian folklore, a huge, mythical bird with golden wings.
KARMA- Action; the law of cause and effect. For every action there is a cause. Good actions lead one closer to perfect happiness or nirvana; bad actions lead one away.
MARA- A Sanskrit word for the evil forces in the world.
MEDITATION- Sitting quietly to focus the mind for inner calmness and peace.
MONASTERY- A place where monks nuns, live, study and worship.
NAGA KING - In Indian folklore, a mythical serpent that lives in the underworld kingdom.
NIRVANA- A state of everlasting joy and peace attained by enlightened holy persons.
OFFERING BOWL- A bowl in which nuns and monks collect offerings of food.
ORDAINED- A monk or nun who has received the full precepts.
PRECEPTS- Moral codes that monks and nuns receive.
RENOUNCE- To give up worldly desires.
SANGHA- The community of Buddhist nuns and monks. The Sanskrit word means "harmonious living."
SANSKRIT- An ancient Indian language. Many sacred Buddhist books are written in Sanskrit.
SPIRITUAL POWERS- The power to see into future and past lives and to transform oneself into various forms.
TUSHITA HEAVEN- The third of the six desire heavens.
UNTOUCHABLES- In ancient times, people in India were divided into classes known as the caste system. Those outside the castes were called outcasts or untouchables. It was against the law for them to touch anyone in a higher caste.

Bibliography

Buddhist Churches of America. **Long Ago in India**. San Francisco, CA: 1987.

Bullard, Sara. "Why Does the Buddha have Long Ears?" Teaching Tolerance. Fall 1998: 28-30.

Cohen, Joan Lebold. **Buddha**. New York: Delacorte Press, 1969.

Demi. **Buddha**. New York: Henry Holt and Co., 1191.

Herbert, Patricia. **The Life of the Buddha.** San Francisco, CA: Pomegranate Art Books, 1993.

Hua, Venerable Master Hsaun. "Life of the Buddha" Taped lecture.

Kassapa and Siridhamm, Venerables. **The Life of the Buddha**. Ceylon: Department of Cultural Affairs, Government Press.

Mahathera, Narada. **The Buddha and his Teachings**. Colombo, Sri Lanka: Lever Brothers, 1987.

Martin, Rafe. **The Tigress**. Berkeley, California: Yellow Moon Press, 1999.

Mitchell, Robert Allen. **The Buddha, His Life Retold**. New York: Paragon House, 1998.

Niwano, Nikkyo. **Shakyamuni Buddha**. Tokyo: Kosei Publishing Co., 1980.

Phangcham, Venerable Dr. C. **Buddhism for Young Students**. Warren, Michigan: Wat Dhammaram.

Phra Khantiplo. **Splendor of Enlightenment**. Bangkok: Mahamakut Rajcundyalaya Press.

Sidsiridhamma, Rev. **The Life of the Buddha**. Jalan Berhala, Kuala Lumpur: Buddhist Missionary Society.

Singapore Buddhist Federation. **Buddhist Studies**. Singapore: Curriculum Development Institute of Singapore, 1984.

Smith, Huston. **The World's Religions**. San Francisco, Ca: Harper, 1991.

The Dharma Realm Buddhist Association

The Dharma Realm Buddhist Association (DRBA) was founded in the United States of America in 1959 by the Venerable Master Hsuan Hua (prior to his own arrival in the U.S.) to bring the genuine teachings of the Buddha to the entire world.

Its goals are to propagate the Proper Dharma, to translate the Mahayana Buddhist scriptures into the world's languages, and to promote ethical education.

The members of the association guide themselves with six ideals established by the Venerable Master which are: no fighting, no greed, no seeking, no selfishness, no pursuing personal advantage, and no lying.

They hold in mind the credo:

Freezing, we do not scheme.
Starving, we do not beg.
Dying of poverty, we ask for nothing.
According with conditions, we do not change.
Not changing, we accord with conditions.
We adhere firmly to our three great principles.
We renounce our lives to do the Buddha's work.
We take responsibility for molding our own destinies.
We rectify our lives to fulfill our role as members of the Sangha.

Encountering specific matters, we understand the principles.
Understanding the principles, we apply them in specific matters.
We carry on the single pulse of the patriarchs' mind-transmission.

During the following decades, international Buddhist communities such as Gold Mountain Monastery, the City of Ten Thousand Buddhas, the City of the Dharma Realm and various other branch facilities were founded. All these operate under the traditions of the Venerable Master and through the auspices of the Dharma Realm Buddhist Association.

Following the guidelines of Shakyamuni Buddha, the Sangha members in these monastic facilities maintain the practices of taking only one meal a day and of always wearing their precept sashes. Reciting the Buddha's name, studying the teachings, and practicing meditation, they dwell together in harmony and personally put the Buddha's teachings into practice.

Reflecting Master Hua's emphasis on translation and education, the association also sponsors an International Translation Institute, vocational training programs for Sangha and laity, the Dharma Realm Buddhist University, and elementary and secondary schools.The Way-places of this association are open to sincere individuals of all races, religions, and nationalities.

Everyone, who is willing to put forth his/her best effort in nurturing humaneness, righteousness, merit, and virtue in order to understand the mind and see the nature, is welcome to join in the study and practice.

Venerable Master Hsuan Hua

The Venerable Master Hsuan Hua was also known as An Tse and To Lun. The name Hsuan Hua was bestowed upon him after he received the transmission of the Wei Yang Lineage of the Chan School from Venerable Elder Hsu Yun. He left the home life at the age of nineteen.

After the death of his mother, he lived in a tiny thatched hut by her grave side for three years, as an act of filial respect. During that time, he practiced meditation and studied the Buddha's teachings. Among his many practices were eating only once a day at midday and never lying down to sleep.

In 1948, the Master arrived in Hong Kong, where he founded the Buddhist Lecture Hall and other monasteries. In 1962, he brought the Proper Dharma to America and to the West, where he lectured extensively on the major works of the Mahayana Buddhist canon and established the Dharma Realm Buddhist Association, as well as the City of Ten Thousand Buddhas, the International Translation Institute, various other monastic facilities, Dharma Realm Buddhist University, Developing Virtue Secondary School, Instilling Goodness Elementary school, the vocational Sangha and Laity Training Programs, and other education centers.

The Master passed into stillness on June 7, 1995, in Los Angeles, U.S.A., causing many people throughout the world to mourn the sudden setting of the sun of wisdom. Although he has passed on, his lofty example will always be remembered. Throughout his life he worked selflessly and vigorously to benefit the people of the world and all living beings. His wisdom and compassion inspired many to correct their faults and lead wholesome lives.

Here we include the Records of the Mendicant of Chang Bai written by the Venerable Master to serve as a model for all of us to emulate.

The Mendicant of Chang Bai was simple and honest in nature.
He was always quick to help people and benefit others.
Forgetting himself for the sake of the Dharma,
he was willing to sacrifice his life.
Bestowing medicines according to people's illnesses,
he offered his own marrow and skin.
His vow was to unite in substance with millions of beings.
His practice-exhausted empty space as
he gathered in the myriad potentials,
Without regard for past, future, or present;
With no distinctions of north, south, east, or west.

Dharma Realm Buddhist Association Branches

Home Page: **http://www.drba.org**

Main Branch:

The City of Ten Thousand Buddhas

4951 Bodhi Way, Ukiah, CA 95482 USA
Tel: (707) 462-0939 Fax: (707) 462-0949

The International Translation Institute
1777 Murchison Drive, Burlingame,
CA 94010-4504 U.S.A.
Tel: (650) 692-5912 Fax: (650) 692-5056

Institute for World Religions
(Berkeley Buddhist Monastery)
2304 McKinley Avenue, Berkeley,
CA 94703 U.S.A.
Tel: (510) 848-3440

Gold Mountain Monastery
800 Sacramento Street, San Francisco,
CA 94108 U.S.A.
Tel: (415) 421-6117

Gold Sage Monastery
11455 Clayton Road, San Jose,
CA 95127 U.S.A.
Tel: (408) 923-7243 Fax: (408) 923-1064

The City of the Dharma Realm
1029 West Capitol Ave., West Sacramento,
CA 95691 U.S.A.
Tel: (916) 374-8268 Fax: (916) 374-8234

Gold Wheel Monastery
235 N. Avenue 58, Los Angeles,
CA 90042 U.S.A.
Tel: (323) 258-6668

Long Beach Monastery
3361 East Ocean Boulevard, Long Beach,
CA 90803 U.S.A.
Tel: (562) 438-8902

Blessings, Prosperity & Longevity Monastery
4140 Long Beach Boulevard, Long Beach,
CA 90807 U.S.A.
Tel: (562) 595-4966

Avatamsaka Vihara
9601 Seven Locks Road
Bethesda, MD 20817
Tel: (301) 469-8300

Gold Summit Monastery
233 Ist Avenue W., Seattle,
WA 98119 U.S.A.
Tel: (206) 284-6690 Fax: (260) 284-6918

Gold Buddha Monastery
248 East 11th Ave., Vancouver, B.C.
V6A lP3 Canada.
Tel: (604) 709-0248 Fax: (604) 684-3754

Avatamsaka Monastery
1009 4th Avenue, S.W. Calgary,
AB T2P OK8 Canada.
Tel: (403) 269-2960

Dharma Realm Buddhist Books Distribution Society
11th Floor, 85 Chung-hsiao E. Road, Sec. 6,
Taipei, Taiwan R.O.C.
Tel: (02) 2786-3022 Fax: (02) 2786-2674

Prajna Guanyin Sagely Monastery
Batu 5 1/2, Jalan Sungai Besi, Salak Selatan
57100 Kuala Lumpur, Malaysia.
Tel: (03) 7982-6560 Fax: (03) 7980-1272

raleigh

Index

Page numbers in italics refer to illustrations.